SUPER SCIENCE

Light and Sound

Experiments

Chris Oxlade

Consultant: John Farndon

Miles
Kelly

CONTENTS

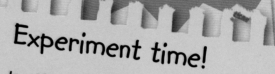

Learn all about light and sound, including how light travels and why we hear sounds.

Experiment time!

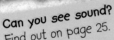

Can you see sound?
Find out on page 25.

Which travels faster, light or sound?
Find out on page 27.

What happens when a light ray hits a mirror?
Find out on page 15.

SUPER SCIENCE

Light and Sound

Experiments

First published in 2011 by Miles Kelly Publishing Ltd
Harding's Barn, Bardfield End Green, Thaxted, Essex, CM6 3PX, UK

2 4 6 8 10 9 7 5 3 1

Publishing Director Belinda Gallagher

Creative Director Jo Cowan

Editors Amanda Askew, Sarah Parkin

Editorial Assistant Lauren White

Senior Designer Joe Jones

Designer Kayleigh Allen

Photographer Simon Pask

Production Manager Elizabeth Collins

Reprographics Anthony Cambray, Stephan Davis, Jennifer Hunt

ISBN 978-1-84810-314-6

Printed in China

British Library Cataloguing-in-Publication Data
A catalogue record for this book is available from the British Library

ACKNOWLEDGEMENTS
The publishers would like to thank the following
sources for the use of their photographs:
Shutterstock.com 6(tr) Ivan Cholakov Gostock-dot-net; 11(c) Yobidaba,
(bl) travis manley, (br) yalayama **Fotolia.com** 7(tr) Andres Rodriguez

Every effort has been made to acknowledge the source and
copyright holder of each picture. Miles Kelly Publishing apologises
for any unintentional errors or omissions.

Miles Kelly Publishing is not responsible for the accuracy or
suitability of the information on any website other than its own.
We recommend that children are supervised while on the Internet
and that they do not use Internet chat rooms.

Made with paper from a sustainable forest

www.mileskelly.net   info@mileskelly.net
www.factsforprojects.com

Notes for HELPERS

Help and hazards

Help needed

- All of the experiments are suitable for children to conduct, but they will need help and supervision with some. This is usually because the experiment requires the use of scissors for cutting. These experiments are marked with a 'Help needed' symbol.

- Read the instructions together before starting and help to assemble the equipment before supervising the experiment.

- It may be useful to carry out your own risk assessment to avoid any possible hazards before your child begins. Check that long hair and any loose clothing are tied back.

- Check that sharp objects such as scissors are put away safely after use.

Extra experiments

Also try...

You can also help your children with the extra experiments in this book, or search the Internet for more, similar ideas. There are hundreds of science experiment websites to choose from.

www.kids-science-experiments.com This website is packed with simple, fun experiments for your children to enjoy.

www.sciencebob.com/experiments/index.php Engaging science experiments with clearly explained instructions will keep your kids busy for hours.

www.tryscience.org You will find lots of entertaining and informative experiments on this colourful, interactive website.

What is LIGHT?

Light is a type of energy that you can see and it is essential for all kinds of things. We need light to grow food and to be able to see around us. In earlier times, people used fires, candles or oil for lighting. Now we make our own light with electricity or gas.

Hot light

Light is usually produced by a very hot object, such as a light bulb or fire, and heat is released. The Sun is our main source of light. Its rays travel through space and reach us as heat and light energy.

Sun

How light travels

Light travels in straight lines, called rays. Light rays change direction if they are reflected off or pass through an object or substance, but they still remain straight.

Viperfish

Cold light

Some animals produce a kind of light that gives off no heat. Fireflies and glow-worms are insects that can make parts of their bodies glow with light. About 1500 different deep-sea fish give off light.

Refraction

When a straw is placed in water, it looks as though it is slightly bent. This is because light rays bend when they pass through water. This bending of rays is called refraction.

Reflection

When light hits a very smooth surface such as a mirror, it reflects (bounces) off the surface. If it hits a mirror at an angle, it is reflected off at exactly the same angle.

The eye receives a reflection of the image

Light rays bounce of the mirror

Actual object

What is SOUND?

Most sounds you hear, from the whisper of the wind to the roar of a jet, are actually moving air. Every sound originates with something vibrating. This makes the air vibrate too, and the vibrations in the air carry the sound to your ears. The vibrations that carry sound through the air are called sound waves.

Inside the ear

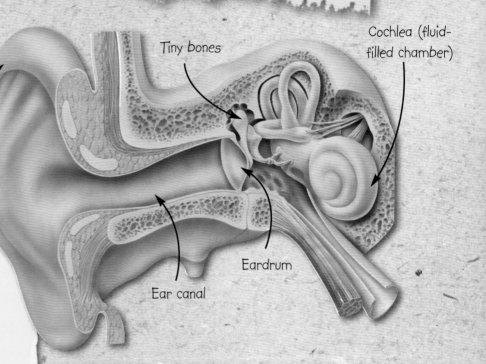

Outer ear

Tiny bones

Cochlea (fluid-filled chamber)

Eardrum

Ear canal

How do we hear sound?

The outer ear funnels sound waves into the ear. From there, sounds pass through a tube called the ear canal to the eardrum. Sounds make the eardrum and tiny bones in the middle ear vibrate. These bones pass the sound to the cochlea, in the inner ear, where nerve cells change the vibrations into messages that travel to the brain, which recognizes what we are hearing.

Rustling leaves: 10 dB

Talking: 40 dB

Thunder: 100 dB

Atom bomb: 210 dB

Sound measurement

The loudness (volume) of sound is measured in decibels (dB). A quiet sound, such as whispering, is 20 dB. A very loud sound, such as a jet plane taking off, is 120 dB.

7

Using this book

Each experiment has numbered instructions and clear explanations about your findings. Read through all the instructions before you start an experiment, and then follow them carefully, one at a time. If you are not sure what to do, ask an adult.

Experiment symbols

① Shows how long the experiment will take once you have collected all the equipment you need.

② Shows if you need to ask an adult to help you with the experiment.

③ Shows how easy or difficult the experiment is to do.

① ② ③

15 min   No help needed   Easy

Introduction
See what you will be learning about in each experiment.

BLOW some music

The clarinet, the trumpet and the recorder are all instruments you blow to move the air and make a sound. Try this experiment to see how these wind instruments work.

You will need
- work surface
- square of card, 10 cm by 10 cm
- double-sided sticky tape
- 20 drinking straws
- scissors

ⓐ Make sure the tape goes right to the edges

Put two strips of double-sided sticky tape across the piece of card at opposite edges. Remove the backing.

Things you will need
You should be able to find the equipment around the house or from a supermarket. No special equipment is needed. Always ask before using materials from home.

Safety
If there is a 'Help needed' symbol at the start of the experiment, you must ask an adult to help you.

The warning symbol also tells you to be careful when using scissors. Always ask an adult for help.

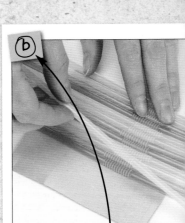

ⓑ With the tape at the top and bottom, pre straws onto the tape side by side. The end straws must line up along the top of the c

30

8

Stages
Numbers and letters guide you through the stages of each experiment.

Labels
Handy labels will provide you with useful tips and information to help your experiment run smoothly.

Explanation
At the end of each experiment is a question-and-answer explanation. It tells you what should have happened and why.

(c)

Make sure the cut ends open up

Diagonally cut off the bottoms of the straws. Cut across so that the first straw is about 10 cm long and the last straw is full length.

Q What sounds do you make?

A The short straws produce higher notes than the long straws. The straws work as tubes. When you blow across the top, the moving air creates vibrations that travel up and down each straw. The harder you blow, the stronger the vibrations grow, so the louder the sounds become. The short straws produce higher notes because the speed of the vibrations depends on the length of the tube – smaller tubes create faster vibrations.

Also try...
Simple mini experiments to test the science you've learnt.

Also try...
Fill glass bottles with different amounts of coloured water. Blow across the tops of the bottles and listen to the different sounds you can make.

(d)

Hold the straw instrument with the t[...] straws near your bottom lip. Blow a[...] to produce sound.

Doing the experiments

✹ Clear a surface to work on, such as a table, and cover it with newspaper if you need to.

✹ You could wear an apron or old t-shirt to protect your clothing.

✹ Gather all the equipment you need before you start, and tidy up after each experiment.

✹ Ask an adult to help you when an experiment is marked with a 'Help needed' or warning symbol.

✹ Work over a tray or sink when you are pouring water.

✹ Always ask an adult to help if you are unsure what to do.

Scientist KIT

Before you begin experimenting you will need to gather some equipment. You should be able to find all of it around the house or from a local supermarket. Ask an adult's permission before using anything and take care when you see a warning sign.

From the Kitchen

- 3 clean, empty jars
- 20 drinking straws
- funnel
- glass or jar with a small opening
- jug
- scissors
- shallow plastic container
- small plate
- teaspoon
- water

Straws

Scissors

Pencils

⚠️ Warning!
Scissors are extremely sharp and can cut you easily. Make sure you ask an adult for help. When passing scissors, always point the handles towards the other person.

Handy hint!
Flour is messy! Make sure you do any experiments involving flour outside.

Flour

Foody things

- flour
- red, green and blue food colouring
- sugar or salt

Handy hint!
Food colouring is very helpful because it allows you to see what is happening in your experiment and shows your results clearly.

Food colouring

Card

From the craft box

- card (white and coloured)
- coloured pencils
- double-sided sticky tape
- large elastic bands
- modelling clay or sticky tack
- 2 pencils or pens, the same thickness
- pins
- short pencil
- stapler
- sticky tape
- thick pen
- thin, white paper
- tracing paper

Pin

Elastic bands

Other stuff

- balloons
- shoe boxes with lids
- small mirror
- torch

Mirror

Torch

Balloons

Handy hint!
It doesn't have to be night-time to experiment in the dark. Just close your curtains and turn off any lights to create darkness.

Places you'll need to work

- large outside space
- wall in a dark room
- work surface

Remember to recycle and re-use

One way to help the environment is by recycling and re-using materials such as glass, paper, plastics and scrap metals. It is mostly cheaper and less wasteful than making new products from stratch.

Re-using means you use materials again in their original form rather than throwing them away.

Recycling is when materials are taken to a plant where they can be melted and re-made into either the same or new products.

Handy hint!
Plastic bottles come in many different colours. Try to use a clear bottle so that you can see your experiment working.

11

Hand SHADOWS

Shadows are made when something blocks light. Try this experiment to make shadows that are big or small, sharp or blurred.

 15 min
 No help needed
 Easy

You will need
- wall in a dark room
- torch or lamp

Preparation

Turn off all the lights and shut the curtains, so the room is as dark as possible. Shine the torch on a wall. Either hold it or rest it on a level surface.

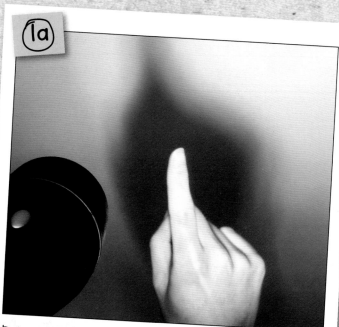

1a

Point your finger upwards and hold it about 5 cm in front of the torch's light.

1b

Watch the shape of the shadow ➔

Move your hand another 5 cm away from the torch.

Q What does the shadow look like

A **It is large and blurred.** Your hand is close to the light source, so it blocks out a wide area of the light beam, making a large shadow. Having a wide light source like a torch close to your hand makes the edges of the shadow blurred.

 12

2a

Move your hand about 20 cm away from the torch.

2b

Then move your hand as far away from the torch and as close to the wall as you can (without touching the wall).

Q How does the shadow change?

A It becomes smaller and sharper. The further away your hand is from the light, the less of the beam your hand stops, so the smaller the shadow. The edges of the shadow are sharper because the light can't get round the edges of your hand.

Also try...

Put on a shadow puppet play. Make some puppets by cutting out card shapes, such as a horse or sheep. Then stick your puppet to a straw or short stick. Put these in front of the torch in the same way as you did with your hand. Start your 'On the Farm' play! Use these shapes to help you.

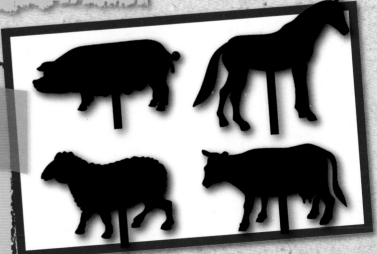

Ray of LIGHT

When you turn on a torch, it produces a ray of light. This experiment shows how light travels only in straight lines.

 30 min   No help needed   Hard

You will need

- work surface
- thin A4 card (any colour)
- scissors
- modelling clay or sticky tack
- torch
- small mirror

Preparation

Make the slit about 2 mm wide

a Carefully cut a piece of A4 card in half. Hold the pieces together and cut a slot 5 cm deep in one of the long edges.

b Stand one of the pieces of card on its slotted edge. Support it with four pieces of sticky tack or modelling clay near the corners.

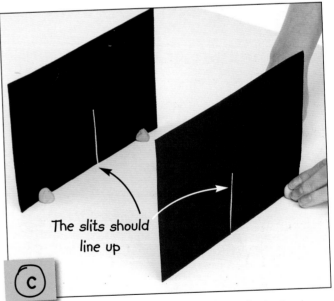

The slits should line up

c Stand the other piece of card on its slotted edge, parallel to the first piece and about 15 cm away from it. Support it with four pieces of modelling clay. The slots in the cards should be roughly opposite each other.

1

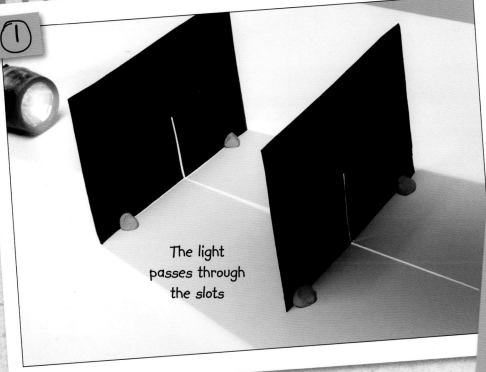

The light passes through the slots

Switch off the lights, or close the curtains to make the room dark. Shine a torch through one of the slots from about 10 cm away. Move the torch from side to side to make the ray pass through both slots.

Q What does the light do?

A The light ray passes through the slots. The light can only pass all the way through when the torch and both slots are all in line with each other. When the torch and slots are not in line, no light goes through the second slot. This shows that light travels only in straight lines.

2

Replace one piece of card with a mirror, with its reflecting side facing the remaining card. Shine the torch through the slot towards the mirror.

Bounce!

Q Does the light stop?

A No, the mirror reflects the light ray. The light ray that hits the mirror bounces back. When you move the torch from side to side, you'll see that the ray always bounces off the mirror at the same angle as it hits.

Through a LENS

In a camera, a glass or plastic lens bends light rays together to make an image that the camera records. Here's how to make a camera that makes a picture with just a simple hole.

30 min   Help needed   Hard

You will need

- work surface
- shoe box with lid
- scissors
- sticky tape
- tracing paper
- torch
- coloured card
- pin

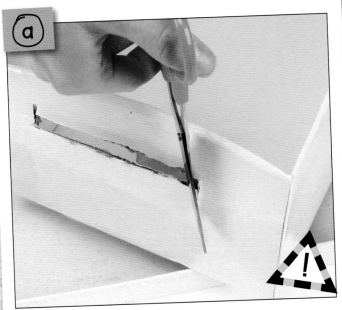

(a)

Carefully cut a hole about 8 cm by 5 cm in the centre of one side of the box.

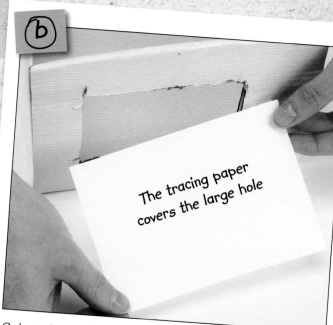

(b)

The tracing paper covers the large hole

Cut a piece of tracing paper about 10 cm by 7 cm. Stick it over the hole in the box, making sure it is not creased.

Push the pin through the box

Carefully push a pin through the box, opposite the first hole, to make a small, round hole.

Turn off any lights and make the room as dark as possible. Hold the box in front of your face with the tracing paper screen closest to you. Aim the box at the torch. If the image is dim, try draping a cloth over your head and the top of the box.

Cut a triangle shape in coloured card and tape it to the front of the torch. Turn on the torch and rest it at head height.

Q What can you see?

A An upside-down triangle! Rays of light coming from the torchlight go through the hole in the box and hit the screen. Light rays travel in straight lines, so rays travelling over the top of the triangle hit the bottom of the screen, and rays going under the bottom of the triangle hit the top of the screen.

Rainbow COLOURS

A rainbow is made when sunlight splits into different colours. Here's how to make these rainbow colours.

You will need

- work surface
- dark room
- shallow plastic container
- water
- jug
- small mirror
- sticky tack
- white card
- torch

(a) Rest a small mirror in one end of the container, angled at about 45 degrees, with the reflecting side facing upwards. Add a small piece of sticky tack to hold the mirror in place.

(b) Half fill the plastic container with water.

Rest the card against a glass or pile of books

(c) Balance a piece of white card on the table at the other end of the plastic container.

(d) Make the room as dark as possible. Turn off the lights, close the curtains and block any light coming into the room.

18

The colours of the rainbow →

The rainbow will appear on the card

(e)

Hold the torch about 10 cm away from the mirror and turn it on. Make sure you shine the light on the mirror underneath the water. Adjust the angle of the torch until you see the colours of the rainbow on the card. What can you see?

Also try...

On a sunny day, stand with your back to the Sun and spray water into the air in front of you. The sunlight is split into colours as it enters and exits the tiny drops of water in the air, making a rainbow.

(Q) **Why can you see a rainbow?**

(A) **Light from a torch and light from the Sun is called white light.** It is made up of many different colours mixed together. The rays of light from the torch go into the water, bounce off the mirror, come out of the water again and hit the card. As the rays go in and out of the water they bend. The different colours bend by slightly different amounts, so they split up and you can see them. These colours are called the colours of the spectrum.

CHANGING colours

In these experiments, you can see how your eyes add colours, and how filters block out colours.

 30 min
 No help needed
 Hard

You will need

- work surface
- white card
- small plate
- short pencil
- scissors
- water
- magneta (dark pink), cyan (blue/green) and yellow coloured pencils
- 3 clean, empty jars
- red, green and blue food colouring

1a

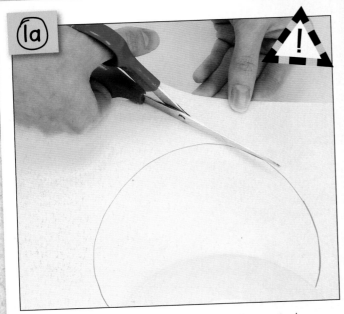

Draw around the small plate to make a circle on the card. Carefully cut out the circle.

1b

Make your colours strong

Draw lines to divide the card into three equal sections. Colour the sections magneta, cyan and yellow.

1c

Push a short, sharp pencil through the centre of the coloured circle. Stand the pencil on its tip on a hard surface and then spin it.

Q Which colour can you see?

A When you spin the spinner, your eyes merge the colours to make white or grey. By mixing cyan, magenta and yellow paints or coloured pencils in different amounts, you can make any colour you like. These special colours are called the primary colours of pigments.

②a

Fill three jars with water. Add several drops of food colouring to each jar (red in one jar, blue in another jar and green in the last jar).

②b

Stand the green jar in front of the other two jars, with a window or other light source behind them. Look through the green jar. What do you see? Then try standing the red and blue jars in front.

Q Which two colours block light?

A Any two of red, green and blue. These are the primary colours of light. The jars are filters. Each one lets through only one colour of light (e.g. the red jar lets through only red light, and blocks green and blue). With two jars together, the colour that goes through the first is blocked by the second (so green light from the green jar is blocked by the red jar).

Only green can be seen

Only red comes ahead

Only blue shows through

21

Picture flicker BOOK

Here's how to make an optical toy that shows how our eyes are fooled into seeing movement on a television or cinema screen.

30 min   No help needed   Easy

a

Trace each image carefully

Draw a clock face on each of the pieces of paper. It must be in exactly the same place and look exactly the same, so trace each one..

You will need

- work surface
- 12 or more small pieces of thin, white paper, about 10 cm by 8 cm
- stapler
- coloured pens or pencils

b

Draw the hands on each clock face

On each piece of paper, change the time by one hour. You should have 12 o'clock, 1 o'clock, 2 o'clock, 3 o'clock, and so on.

c

The time should start at
12 o'clock and then
count on, hour by hour

Staple the pieces of paper together, making sure they are in the right order.

Also try...

Try drawing more difficult images with more than 12 pieces of paper.

d

Now flick the pages from start to finish whilst watching the clock faces.

Q What makes the image appear to be moving?

A The pictures on the pages pass in front of your eyes one after the other, in quick succession, each for a split second. Your brain remembers each image for a short time, so you get the impression of a moving clock hand. Television and films work in the same way, showing images in quick succession on the screen.

Seeing SOUND

You can't actually see sound as it travels through the air. But here's an experiment that lets you see the vibrations that sound is made from.

15 min   No help needed   Easy

You will need

- work surface
- balloon
- scissors
- glass or jar with a small opening
- sticky tape
- sugar or salt

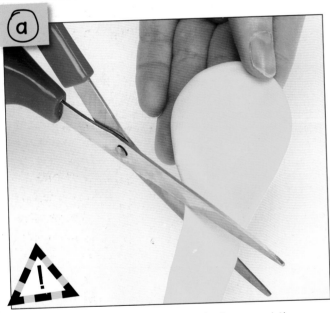

a

Carefully cut off the neck of a balloon and throw it away.

b

Your glass should have a small opening to fit the balloon over

Put the body of the balloon over the top of a glass. Stretch it to make a tight skin, like that on a drum.

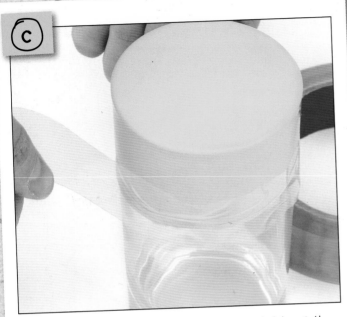

c

Wrap some sticky tape around the outside of the glass to keep the edge of the balloon in place.

e

Hmmmmm!

With your mouth about 10 cm from the balloon's surface, hum loudly. Also try humming a high note and a low note.

d

Stand the glass on a table and put a few grains of salt or sugar on the balloon skin.

Q Do the grains on the balloon move?

A Yes! Sound is made up of vibrations that move through the air. The vibrations are called sound waves. When something makes a sound, vibrations spread out from it into the air in all directions. When the vibrations in the air hit something they make it vibrate, too. When sound waves from your mouth hit the stretched balloon, they make it vibrate up and down, which you can see because the grains jump up and down.

LIGHT races sound

You hear sounds as soon as they are made. That's because sound travels really fast. Here's an experiment to prove it.

15 min   Help needed   Easy

You will need
- large outside space
- balloon
- flour
- funnel
- teaspoon
- pin
- helper

a Put the neck of a balloon over the funnel.

b Add the flour one spoonful at a time

Add a few spoonfuls of flour into the funnel and shake it down into the balloon.

c Remove the funnel, inflate the balloon and tie the neck to stop the air and flour from escaping. Don't inhale when blowing up the balloon – you'll get flour in your mouth.

A You should have seen the balloon burst, just before you heard the bang. This shows that light travels faster than sound. Light won the race easily. In fact, the difference in speeds is huge. Light travels at a staggering 300,000,000 metres a second – so fast that you see the balloon burst as it happens. Sound travels at just 340 metres a second. Its journey from the balloon will have taken just over half a second.

d Go outside to your large open space. Your helper should hold the balloon and a pin. Walk 100 large paces away from them.

e Ask your helper to hold the balloon away from their body. Look at the balloon and signal for your helper to pop it. Watch and listen very carefully – you will hear the balloon pop and see the flour escape.

Bang!

Musical BOX

The guitar and violin are both string instruments. Here's an experiment to see how strings make musical notes.

You will need

- work surface
- shoe box with lid
- scissors
- 2 pencils or pens, the same thickness
- thick pen
- large elastic bands

Preparation

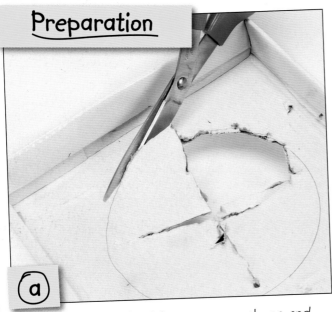

a Cut a round hole about 15 cm across at one end of the box lid. Put the lid back on the box.

b Stretch a few elastic bands lengthways around the box so that they run across the centre of the hole.

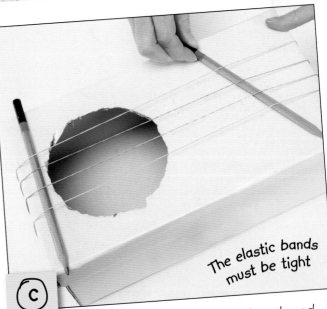

The elastic bands must be tight

c Put a pencil under the elastic bands at each end of the box. The pencils should lift the elastic bands clear of the hole.

① Ping! Ping!

Pluck the elastic bands to make sounds. Pluck the bands hard to make loud sounds and softly to make quieter sounds.

Ⓠ Can you make sound?

Ⓐ Yes because the elastic bands act as the string would on a guitar. When you pluck them, they vibrate from side to side. This vibrates the air around the strings, and you hear the vibrations as sound. The harder you pluck the strings, the stronger the vibrations are. Stronger vibrations make stronger sound waves, which sound louder. The box helps to make the sound louder because the sound bounces around inside it.

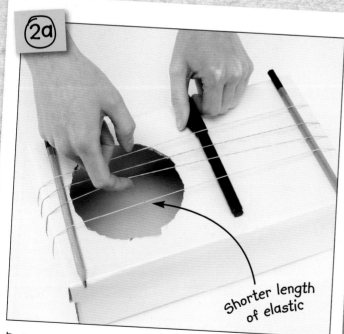

②a

Shorter length of elastic

Put a pen thicker than the pencils under the bands close to the hole. Pluck the bands again.

②b

Try moving the pen backwards and forwards to play different notes.

Ⓠ Does the sound get higher?

Ⓐ Yes, because the pen changes the length of the elastic bands that can vibrate freely. The shorter this is, the faster the bands vibrate, and the higher the notes they make.

BLOW
some music

The clarinet, the trumpet and the recorder are all instruments you blow to move the air and make a sound. Try this experiment to see how these wind instruments work.

15 min   No help needed   Easy

You will need

- work surface
- square of card, 10 cm by 10 cm
- double-sided sticky tape
- 20 drinking straws
- scissors

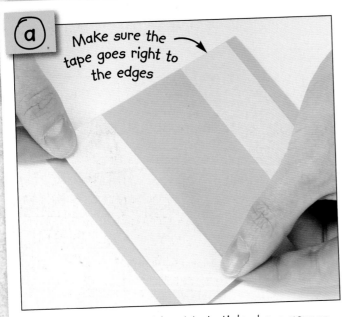

(a) Make sure the tape goes right to the edges

Put two strips of double-sided sticky tape across the piece of card at opposite edges. Remove the backing.

(b)

With the tape at the top and bottom, press the straws onto the tape side by side. The ends of the straws must line up along the top of the card.

c

Make sure the cut ends open up

Diagonally cut off the bottoms of the straws. Cut across so that the first straw is about 10 cm long and the last straw is full length.

A The short straws produce higher notes than the long straws. The straws work as tubes. When you blow across the top, the moving air creates vibrations that travel up and down each straw. The harder you blow, the stronger the vibrations grow, so the louder the sounds become. The short straws produce higher notes because the speed of the vibrations depends on the length of the tube – smaller tubes create faster vibrations.

d

Hold the straw instrument with the tops of the straws near your bottom lip. Blow across the tops to produce sound.

Also try...

Fill glass bottles with different amounts of coloured water. Blow across the tops of the bottles and listen to the different sounds you can make.

RECORD
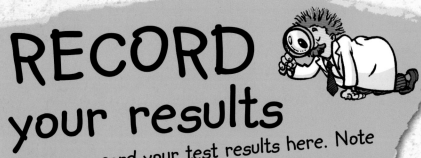
your results

You can record your test results here. Note down how successful the experiments were and what you have learnt about science from them. You could also write about how much you enjoyed each activity.

Add a picture of yourself as a scientist!

Quiz ZONE

Get ready to test how much you've learnt from the experiments in this book. Write down your answers on a piece of paper and then check them against the answers on page 40. No cheating!

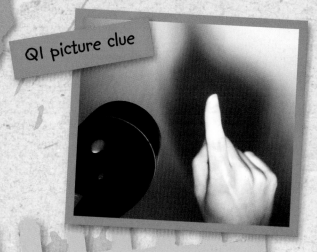

Q1 picture clue

What are the missing words?

1. Shadows are made when ... is blocked.

2. Smaller tubes create ... vibrations than longer tubes.

3. The loudness (volume) of sound is measured in ... .

4. Red, green and blue are known as the ... colours of light.

5. Light from a torch and light from the Sun is called ... .

What word beginning with...

6. V carry sound to your ears?

7. R is made when white light splits into different colours?

Q7 picture c

8. S is our main source of light?

9. R describes what a mirror does to a light ray?

36

True or false?

(10) Light rays always bounce off mirrors at different angles.

(11) Light travels only in straight lines.

(12) Long straws produce higher notes than short straws.

QII picture clue

Multiple choice

(13) If you blow into a straw and gradually increase how hard you blow, what will happen to the volume? It will get louder, it will stay same the same, or it will get quieter?

(14) Does sound travel really fast, really slowly, or not at all?

(15) Which would win in a race – light or sound?

(16) Light rays bend when they pass through water – is this called reflection, retention or refraction?

Remember, remember

(17) What kind of light gives off no heat?

(18) How many metres does sound travel in a second?

Q19 picture clue

(19) Can we see sound?

(20) Which part of your body collects sounds in the air?

More questions this way

PICTURE Quiz

21 In which of the following is the hand closest to the light?

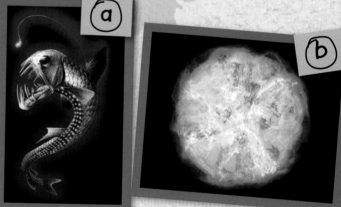

22 Which box makes a higher sound when the elastic bands are plucked?

23 Which of the following produces light that gives off no heat?

24 Which arrangement of jars only lets green light through?

25 In which photograph is the light ray being reflected?

GLOSSARY

ngle The space between two straight lines or
rfaces that join each other, usually measured
degrees.

old light A kind of light that gives off no
at.

olours of the spectrum The rainbow
lours you see when white light is broken up.

ecibel (dB) A unit for measuring the
udness (volume) of sound.

lter A piece of equipment that allows only
rtain things to pass through it.

ot light The light that is produced by a
ry hot object, such as the Sun. Heat is also
leased.

flate To fill something with air or gas so it
comes larger (expands).

ght rays The straight lines that light
avels in.

lerge To combine or join things together to
rm one thing.

ptical Relating to machines or processes to
with light, images or the way we see things.

imary colours of light Blue, green and
d are known as the primary colours of light.

ainbow Made when white light splits into
fferent colours.

Recycling When materials are taken to a
plant where they can be melted and re-made
into either the same or new products.

Reflection When light hits a very smooth
surface and bounces off it.

Refraction The bending of light rays when
they pass through a substance, such as water.

Re-using Using materials again in their
original form rather than throwing them away.

Shadow A dark patch on a surface that is
produced when something blocks light.

Sound waves The vibrations in the air that
carry sound to your ears.

Vibrate To move, or cause to move, a short
distance quickly and continuously.

White light Light that is made up of many
different colours mixed together, such as light
from the Sun.

39

INDEX

QUIZ answers

1. Light 2. Faster 3. Decibels (dB) 4. Primary 5. White light 6. Vibrations 7. Rainbow 8. Sun 9. Reflects 10. False 11. True 12. False 13. False 14. Really fast 15. Light 16. Refraction 17. Cold light 18. 340 metres 19. We can't see sound as it travels through the air, but it is possible to see the vibrations that sound is made from 20. The outer ear 21. c 22. a 23. a 24. b 25. a